Contents

bobble star afghan

Materials

Yarn (4)

...C Essentials, 6oz/170g skeins, each approx 312yd/285m
(...crylic)
...5 skeins #2332 Linen

Hooks

...Size I/9 (5.5mm) crochet hook
...Size K/10½ (6.5mm) crochet hook *or any size to obtain correct gauge*

Additional

• Yarn needle

Measurements

Approx 48"/122cm x 48"/122cm

Gauge

Rounds 1 and 2 = 4"/10cm diameter.

Motif = 15"/38cm square

■■■▢

Stitch Glossary

...ginning PC (beginning popcorn) Ch 3,
...dc in same ch as joining, drop loop from
...ok, insert hook in 3rd ch of beginning
...-3, pull dropped loop through.

...C (popcorn) Work 5 dc in specified st
...sp, drop loop from hook, insert hook in
...st dc, pull dropped loop through.

...v sc (reverse sc) Working from left to
...ht, insert hook in next st to right of last
... yarn over and draw up a loop, yarn over
...d draw through 2 loops on hook.

Afghan

...st Motif

...th K hook, ch 6; join with sl st to form
...ing.

...und 1 (right side) Ch 3 (counts as dc),
...rk 15 dc in ring; join with sl st in 3rd ch
... beginning ch-3—16 dc.

...und 2 Ch 6 (counts as dc and ch-3 sp),
... in same ch as joining; *ch 2, sk next
..., (dc, ch 3, dc) in next dc; re-peat from
...around; ch 2, sk next dc; join with sl st
...3rd ch of beginning ch-6—16 dc, 8 ch-3
...s and 8 ch-2 sps.

...und 3 Sl st in next ch-3 sp, work begin-
...g PC in same ch-3 sp; *ch 2, dc in next
...-2 sp, ch 2**; PC in next ch-3 sp; repeat
...m * around, ending last repeat at **;
...n with sl st in top of beginning PC—8
..., 8 dc and 16 ch-2 sps.

...und 4 Sl st in next ch-2 sp, work begin-
...g PC in same ch-2 sp; *ch 2, dc in next
...**; [ch 2, PC in next ch-2 sp] twice;
...peat from * around, ending last repeat at
...; ch 2, PC in next ch-2 sp, ch 2; join—16
..., 8 dc and 24 ch-2 sps.

...und 5 Sl st in next ch-2 sp, work begin-

ning PC in same ch-2 sp; *ch 2, dc in next
dc**; [ch 2, PC in next ch-2 sp] 3 times;
repeat from * around, ending last repeat at
**; [ch 2, PC in next ch-2 sp] 2 times, ch 2;
join—24 PC, 8 dc and 32 ch-2 sps.

Round 6 Sl st in next ch-2 sp, work beginning PC in same ch-2 sp; *ch 2, dc in next
dc**; [ch 2, PC in next ch-2 sp] 4 times;
repeat from * around, ending last repeat at
**; [ch 2, PC in next ch-2 sp] 3 times, ch 2;
join—32 PC, 8 dc and 40 ch-2 sps.

Round 7 Sl st in next 2 chs and in next dc,
ch 3 (counts as dc), 2 dc in same dc; *ch
4, sk next ch-2 sp, [PC in next ch-2 sp, ch
2] twice, PC in next ch-2 sp, ch 4, sk next
ch-2 sp**; sc in next dc; repeat from * to
** once; 3 dc in next dc; repeat from *
around, ending last repeat at **; join with
sl st in 3rd ch of beginning ch-3—24 PC,
12 dc, 4 sc, 16 ch-4 sps and 16 ch-2 sps.

Round 8 Ch 3 (counts as dc), dc in same
ch as joining; *(tr, ch 2, tr) in next dc, 2 dc
in next dc; **ch 5, PC in next ch-2 sp, ch
2, PC in next ch-2 sp**; [ch 5, sc in next
ch-4 sp] twice; repeat from ** to ** once;
ch 5***; 2 dc in next dc; repeat from *
around, ending last repeat at ***; join—16
PC, 8 tr, 16 dc, 8 sc, 20 ch-5 sps and 12
ch-2 sps .

Round 9 Sl st in next dc, tr and ch-2 sp,
ch 3 (counts as dc), (dc, tr, ch 2, tr, 2 dc) in
same ch-2 sp; *ch 5, sc in next ch-5 sp, ch
5, PC in next ch-2 sp, [ch 5, sc in next ch-5
sp] 3 times, ch 5, PC in next ch-2 sp, ch 5,
sc in next ch-5 sp, ch 5**; (2 dc, tr, ch 2, tr,
2 dc) in next ch-2 sp; repeat from* around,
ending last repeat at **; join—8 PC, 8 tr,
16 dc, 20 sc, 32 ch-5 sps and 4 ch-2 sps.

Round 10 Sl st in next dc, tr and ch-2 sp,
ch 3 (counts as dc), (dc, tr, ch 2, tr, 2 dc) in
same ch-2 sp; *[ch 5, sc in next ch-5 sp]
8 times, ch 5**; (2 dc, tr, ch 2, tr, 2 dc) in

next ch-2 sp; repeat from* around, ending
last repeat at **; join—8 tr, 16 dc, 32 sc,
36 ch-5 sps and 4 ch-2 sps. Fasten off.

Motifs 2—9

Rounds 1–9 Work same as Rounds 1—9
on First Motif.

Note See "Assembly" before working
Round 10. Each motif will have either one-
side or two-side joining.

One-side joining

Round 10 Sl st in next dc, tr and ch-2 sp,
ch 3 (counts as dc), (dc, tr, ch 2, tr, 2 dc) in
same ch-2 sp; [ch 5, sc in next ch-5 sp] 8
times, ch 5, (2 dc, tr, ch 2, tr, 2 dc) in next
ch-2 sp; [ch 5, sc in next ch-5 sp] 8 times,
ch 5; *(2 dc, tr) in next ch-2 sp on current
motif, ch 1, sl st in corresponding ch-2 sp
on adjacent motif, ch 1, (tr, 2 dc) in same
ch-2 sp on current motif**; [ch 2, sl st in
next ch-5 sp on adjacent motif, ch 2, sc in
next ch-5 sp on current motif] 8 times, ch
2, sl st in next ch-5 sp on adjacent motif,
ch 2; repeat from * to ** once; [ch 5, sc in
next ch-5 sp] 8 times, ch 5; join.

Two-side joining

Round 10 Sl st in next dc, tr and ch-2 sp,
ch 3 (counts as dc), (dc, tr, ch 2, tr, 2 dc) in
same ch-2 sp; [ch 5, sc in next ch-5 sp] 8
times, ch 5; *(2 dc, tr) in next ch-2 sp on
current motif, ch 1, sl st in corresponding
ch-2 sp on adjacent motif, ch 1, (tr, 2 dc)
in same ch-2 sp on current motif**; [ch
2, sl st in next ch-5 sp on adjacent motif,
ch 2, sc in next ch-5 sp on current motif]
8 times, ch 2, sl st in next ch-5 sp on
adjacent motif, ch 2; repeat from * once;
repeat from * to ** once; [ch 5, sc in next
ch-5 sp] 8 times, ch 5; join.

bobble star afghan

Assembly

Join motifs in Round 10 into 3 rows with 3 motifs in each row, working one-side or two-side joining as needed, making sure right side of each motif is facing.

Edging

Round 1 With right side facing and I hook, join with sl st in any corner ch-2 sp, ch 1, 3 sc in same corner ch-2 sp; *sc in next 3 sts, [4 sc in next ch-5 sp, sc in next sc, 3 sc in next ch-5 sp, sc in next sc] 4 times, 4 sc in next ch-5 sp, sc in next 3 sts**; sc in next 2 joined ch-2 sps; repeat from * 2 more times, ending last repeat at **; 3 sc in next corner ch-2 sp; repeat from *

3 more times, eliminating last 3 sc on last repeat; join with sl st in first sc—580 sc.
Round 2 Sl st in next sc, ch 2 (counts as hdc), 2 hdc in same sc, hdc in each sc around, working 3 hdc in center sc of 3 sc in each corner; join with sl st in 2nd ch of beginning ch-2—588 hdc. **Note** Corner is worked in 3rd st of 3 sts in corner (instead of in 2nd st of 3 sts in corner) in round 3 to compensate for hdc sts leaning to right.
Round 3 Sl st in next 2 hdc, ch 2 (counts as hdc); 2 hdc in same hdc; *[PC in next hdc, hdc in next 3 hdc] 36 times, PC in next hdc, hdc in next hdc**; 3 hdc in next hdc for corner; repeat from * around, ending last repeat at **; hdc in next hdc;

join—148 PC and 448 hdc.
Round 4 Sl st in next hdc, ch 2 (counts a[s] hdc), 2 hdc in same hdc, hdc in each hdc around, working 3 hdc in center hdc of 3 hdc in each corner; join—604 hdc.
Round 5 Ch 1, sc in same ch as joining; *rev sc in next hdc to right of last st; repeat from * around; join—604 rev sc. Fasten off.

Stitch Diagram

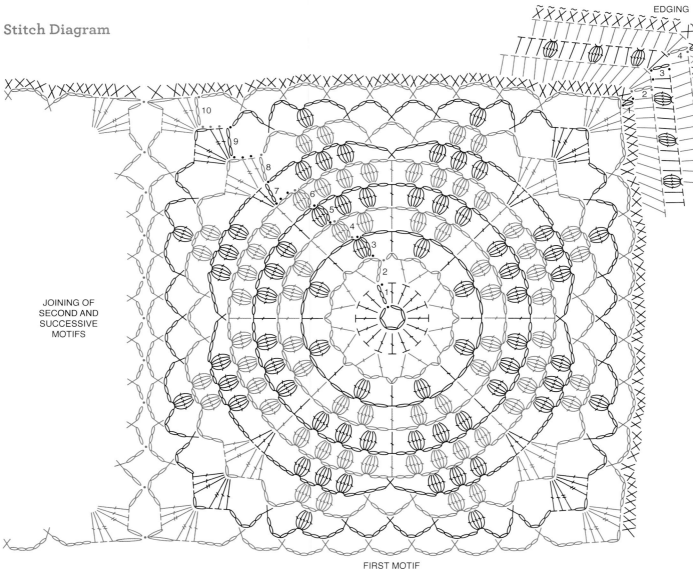

JOINING OF SECOND AND SUCCESSIVE MOTIFS

EDGING

FIRST MOTIF

airy spring throw

Materials

Yarn (4)

RED HEART *Eco-Ways*, 4oz/113g skeins, each approx
186yd/170m (acrylic/recycled polyester)

• 9 skeins #1615 Lichen

Hooks

• Size H/8 (5mm) crochet hook *or any size to obtain correct gauge*
• Size J/10 (6mm) crochet hook

Additional

• Tapestry needle

Measurements

Approx 52"/132cm x 65"/165cm

Gauge

With H hook, 2½ pattern repeats = 6"/15cm; 6 rows = 3"/7.5cm
Remember to check gauge for best results!

How To Make A Gauge Swatch

With H hook, ch 22.
Work same as Rows 1—6. At end of Row 1—2 V-sts. Swatch
should measure approx 6"/15cm wide x 3"/7.5cm high.
Adjust hook size if necessary to obtain correct gauge.

■■□▢▢

Stitch Glossary

V-st (V stitch) (Dc, ch 2, dc) in specified
st or sp.

Shell 5 dc in specified sp.

Afghan

With H hook, ch 172.

Row 1 (right side) Sc in 2nd ch from hook
and in next ch; * ch 3, sk next 3 chs, V-st
in next ch, ch 3, sk next 3 chs**; sc in
next 3 chs; repeat from * across, ending
last repeat at **; sc in last 2 chs-17 V-sts.

Row 2 Ch 1, turn; sc in first sc; * ch 4, sk
next sc, shell in ch-2 sp of next V-st, ch
4, sk next sc, sc in next sc; repeat from *
across—17 shells.

Row 3 Ch 7 (counts as tr and ch-3 sp),
turn; sc in next 5 dc; * ch 7, sc in next 5
dc; repeat from * across; ch 3, tr in last
dc—16 ch-7 sps.

Row 4 Ch 3 (counts as dc now and
throughout), turn; dc in first tr; * ch 3, sk
next sc, sc in next 3 sc, ch 3, sk next sc**;
V-st in next ch-7 sp; repeat from * across,
ending last repeat at **; 2 dc in 4th ch of
beginning ch-7—16 V-sts.

Row 5 Ch 3, turn; 2 dc in first dc, sk next
dc; * ch 4, sk next sc, sc in next sc, ch 4,
sk next sc**; shell in ch-2 sp of next V-st;
repeat from * across, ending last repeat at
**; sk next dc, 3 dc in 3rd ch of beginning
ch-3—16 shells.

Row 6 Ch 1, turn; sc in first 3 dc; * ch 7,
sc in next 5 dc; repeat from * across; ch 7,
sc in last 3 dc—17 ch-7 sps.

Row 7 Ch 1, turn; sc in first 2 sc; * ch 3,
sk next sc, V-st in next ch-7 sp, ch 3, sk

next sc**; sc in next 3 sc; repeat from *
across, ending last repeat at **; sc in last
2 sc—17 V-sts.

Rows 8–101 Repeat Rows 2—7, 15 more
times, then repeat Rows 2—5 once more.

Row 102 Ch 1, turn; sc in first 3 dc; * ch
7, sk next dc, sc in next 3 dc, sk next dc;
repeat from * across; ch 7, sc in last 3
dc—17 ch-7 sps. Do not fasten off.

Edging

Round 1 (right side) Ch 1, turn; 3 sc in first
sc (corner made), sc in next sc, sk next
sc, work [5 sc in each ch-7 sp and sc in
each sc] across to last 3 sc, working 4 sc
(instead of 5 sc) in 3rd, 7th, 11th and 15th
ch-7 sps; sk next sc, sc in next sc, 3 sc in
last sc (corner made); working along side
edge, [sc in edge of each sc, 2 sc in edge
of each dc, 3 sc in edge of each tr] across,
working 4 sc (instead of 3 sc) in edge of
9th tr on side; working in free lps of chs
along bottom edge, 3 sc in first ch (corner
made), [2 sc in each ch-sp, sc in ch at base
of each V-st, sc in ch at base of each sc]
across, skipping ch (instead of working sc
in ch) at base of 6th and 12th V-sts, 3 sc
in last st (corner made); work side edge
same as other side edge; join with sl st in
first sc—616 sc (131 sc on top and bottom
edges, 171 sc on each side edge and 3 sc
in each corner).

Note

Center sc of 3 sc in each corner on round
1 is corner sc.

Round 2 With J hook, sl st in next sc, ch
4 (counts as dc and ch-1 sp), ([dc, ch 1]
twice, dc) in same sc; * [ch 1, sk next sc,
dc in next sc] across to next corner, ch 1,

Rose Callahan

sk next sc ** ; ([dc, ch 1] 3 times, dc) in
next corner sc; repeat from * around, ending last repeat at **; join with sl st in 3rd
ch of beginning ch-4.

Round 3 Sl st in next ch and in next dc, sl
st in next ch-1 sp, ch 6 (counts as dc and
ch-3 sp), dc in same ch-1 sp; * ch 3, sk
next 2 dc, sc in next dc, [sc in next ch-1
sp, sc in next dc] 5 times, ch 3, sk next 2
ch-1 sps ** ; (dc, ch 3, dc) in next ch-1 sp;
repeat from * around, ending last repeat
at ** ; join with sl st in 3rd ch of beginning
ch-6.

Note

Center ch-sp in each corner on round 3
should have (dc, ch 3, dc) worked in it.

Round 4 Ch 4 (counts as dc and ch-1 sp
now and throughout); *(dc, ch 3, dc) in
next ch-3 sp, ch 1, dc in next dc, ch 3,
sk next sc, sc in next 9 sc, ch 3, sk next
sc **; dc in next dc, ch 1; repeat from *

airy spring throw

round, ending last repeat at ** ; join with sl st in 3rd ch of beginning ch-4.

Round 5 Ch 4, dc in next dc, ch 1; * (dc, ch 3, dc) in next ch-3 sp, [ch 1, dc in next dc] twice, ch 3, sk next sc, sc in next 7 sc, ch 3, sk next sc ** ; [dc in next dc, ch 1] twice; repeat from * around, ending last repeat at **; join.

Round 6 Ch 4, [dc in next dc, ch 1] twice; * (dc, ch 3, dc) in next ch-3 sp, [ch 1, dc in next dc] 3 times, ch 3, sk next sc, sc in next 5 sc, ch 3, sk next sc** ; [dc in next dc, ch 1] 3 times; repeat from * around, ending last repeat at **; join.

Round 7 Ch 4, [dc in next dc, ch 1] 3 times; * (dc, ch 3, dc) in

next ch-3 sp, [ch 1, dc in next dc] 4 times, ch 3, sk next sc, sc in next 3 sc, ch 3, sk next sc ** ; [dc in next dc, ch 1] 4 times; repeat from * around, ending last repeat at ** ; join.

Round 8 Ch 1, sc in same ch as joining; * [ch 3, sc in next dc] 4 times, ch 3, sc in next ch-3 sp, [ch 3, sc in next dc] 5 times, ch 4, sl st in 3rd ch from hook (picot made), ch 1** ; sc in next dc; repeat from * around, ending last repeat at **; join with sl st in first sc. Fasten off.

Finishing

Weave in ends.

Stitch Diagram

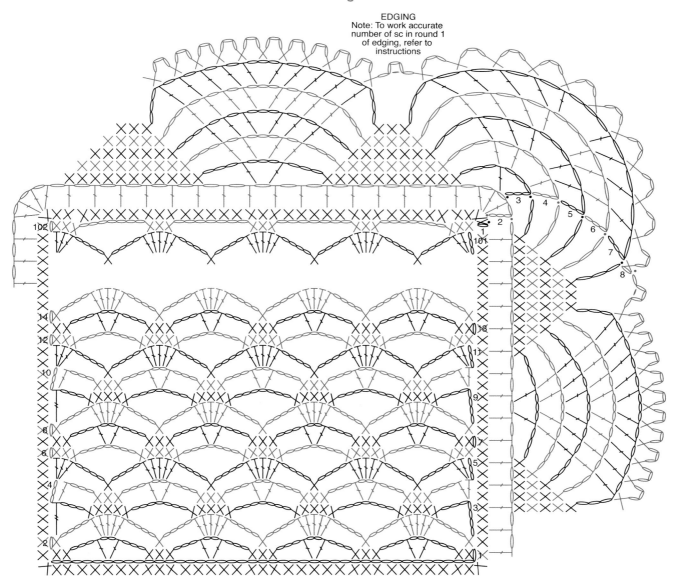

EDGING
Note: To work accurate number of sc in round 1 of edging, refer to instructions

■ ■ ■ ▭

Stitch Glossary

ch chain
dc double crochet
rev sc reverse single crochet
sc single crochet
sk skip
sl st slip stitch
st(s) stitch(es)
* Repeat directions following * as many times as indicated

Notes

1 To create mosaic effect, work all doubl[e] crochet stitches in front of the ch-2 spaces.
2 Each ch-2 space counts as a single stitch, throughout.
3 To change color, work last yarn over of old color to last yarn over; yarn over with new color and draw through all loops on hook to complete stitch. Proceed working with new color.

Afghan

With A, ch 136.

Row 1 (right side) Sc in 2nd ch from hoo[k] and in each remaining ch across—135 sc.
Row 2 Ch 1, turn, sc in each sc across; change to B in last st.
Row 3 Ch 1, turn, sc in first 3 sc, *ch 2, sk next sc, sc in next sc, ch 2, sk next s[c,] sc in next 3 sc; repeat from * across—9[1] sc and 44 ch-spaces.
Row 4 Ch 1, turn, sc in first 3 sc, *ch 2, sk next ch-2 space, sc in next sc, ch 2, s[k] next ch-2 space, sc in next 3 sc; repeat from * across; change to A in last sc.
Row 5 Ch 1, turn, sc in first 2 sc, *ch 2, sk next sc, dc in next skipped st 3 rows below, sc in next sc, dc in next skipped st 3 rows below, ch 2, sk next sc, sc in next sc; repeat from * to last sc, sc in las[t] sc—47 sc, 44 dc, and 44 ch-spaces.
Row 6 Ch 1, turn, sc in first 2 sc, *ch 2, sk next ch-2 space, sc in next 3 sts, ch 2[,] sk next ch-2 space, sc in next sc; repeat from * to last sc, sc in last sc; change to B in last sc—91 sc and 44 ch-spaces.
Row 7 Ch 1, turn, sc in first sc, *ch 2, sk next sc, dc in next skipped st 3 rows below, sc in next 3 sc, dc in next skippe[d] st 3 rows below; repeat from * to last 2 sc, ch 2, sk next sc, sc in last sc—68 sc, 44 dc, and 23 ch-spaces.
Row 8 Ch 1, turn, sc in first sc, *ch 2, sk

beach blanket

Materials

Yarn (4)

RED HEART *Soft Yarn,* 5oz/140g balls, each approx 256yd/234m
(acrylic)

6 balls #9520 Seafoam (A)
6 balls #9518 Teal (B)

Hook

Size I/9 (5.5mm) crochet hook *or any size to obtain correct gauge*

Additional

Yarn needle

Measurements

Approx 50"/127cm wide x 60"/152.5cm long

Gauge

11 sts and 12 rows = 4"/10cm over mosaic pattern as established
using size I/9 (5.5mm) crochet hook.
Remember to check gauge for best results!

How to make a gauge swatch

Ch 34, work Rows 1 through 12 of afghan instructions (below).
Resulting gauge swatch should measure approx 12" x 4"/30.5cm x
10cm. Adjust hook size if necessary to obtain correct gauge.

---

next ch-2 space, sc in next 5 sts; repeat from * to last ch-2 space,
ch 2, sk next ch-2 space, sc in last sc; change to A in last sc—112
sc and 23 ch-spaces.

Row 9 Ch 1, turn, sc in first sc, *dc in next skipped st 3 rows below, sc in next 2 sc, ch 2, sk next sc, sc in next 2 sc; repeat from
* to last ch-2 space, dc in next skipped st 3 rows below, sc in last
sc—90 sc, 23 dc, and 22 ch-spaces.

Row 10 Ch 1, turn, sc in first 4 sts, *ch 2, sk next ch-2 space, sc
in next 5 sts; repeat from * to last ch-2 space, ch 2, sk next ch-2
space, sc in last 4 sts; change to B in last sc—113 sc and 22 ch-
spaces.

Row 11 Ch 1, turn, sc in first sc, *ch 2, sk next sc, sc in next 2
sc, dc in next skipped st 3 rows below, sc in next 2 sc; repeat
from * to last 2 sc, ch 2, sk next sc, sc in last sc—90 sc, 22 dc,
and 23 ch-spaces.

Row 12 Ch 1, turn, sc in first sc, *ch 2, sk next ch-2 space, sc
in next 5 sts; repeat from * to last ch-2 space, ch 2, sk next ch-2

space, sc in last sc; change to A in last sc—112 sc and 23 ch-
spaces.

Row 13 Ch 1, turn, sc in first sc, *dc in next skipped st 3 rows
below, ch 2, sk next sc, sc in next 3 sc, ch 2, sk next sc; repeat
from * to last ch-2 space, dc in next skipped st 3 rows below, sc
in last sc—68 sc, 23 dc, and 44 ch-spaces.

Row 14 Ch 1, turn, sc in first 2 sts, *ch 2, sk next ch-2 space, sc
in next 3 sc, ch 2, sk next ch-2 space, sc in next st; repeat from
* to last sc, sc in last sc; change to B in last st—91 sc and 44
ch-spaces.

Row 15 Ch 1, turn, sc in first 2 sc, *dc in next skipped st 3 rows
below, ch 2, sk next sc, sc in next sc, ch 2, sk next sc, dc in next
skipped st 3 rows below, sc in next sc; repeat from * to last sc,
sc in last sc—47 sc, 44 dc, and 44 ch-spaces.

Row 16 Ch 1, turn, sc in first 3 sts, *ch 2, sk next ch-2 space, sc
in next sc, ch 2, sk next ch-2 space, sc in next 3 sts; repeat from
*across; change to A in last st—91 sc and 44 ch-spaces.

Row 17 Ch 1, turn, sc in first 3 sc, *dc in next skipped st 3 rows
below, sc in next sc, dc in next skipped st 3 rows below, sc in
next 3 sts; repeat from * across.

Row 18 Ch 1, turn, sc in each st across; change to B in last
st—135 sc.

Repeat Rows 3—18 until piece measures approx 60"/152.5cm
from beginning, end after working a Row 18; change to A in last
st of last row. Do not fasten off.

Finishing

Border

Round 1 (right side) With A, ch 1, sc evenly spaced around all
edges of afghan, working 3 sc in each corner; join with sl st in
first sc.

Round 2 Ch 1, rev sc in each st around; join with sl st in first sc.
Fasten off.

Weave in all ends.

oversized argyles

Materials

Yarn 4

TLC *Cotton Plus*, 3.5oz/100g balls, each approx 186yds/170m (cotton/acrylic)
• 9 balls #3811 Medium Blue (A)
• 3 balls #3643 Kiwi (B)
• 2 balls #3100 Cream (C)
• 1 ball #3859 Navy (D)

Hook

Size I/9 (6mm) crochet hook *or any size to obtain correct gauge*

Additional

• Yarn needle

Measurements

Approx 51"/129.5cm wide x 66"/167.5cm long

Gauge

14 hdc + 10 rows = 4"/10cm using size I/9 (6mm) crochet hook. *Remember to check gauge for best results!*

How to make a gauge swatch

Ch 16.

Row 1 Hdc in 3rd ch from hook and each ch across—14 hdc.
Rows 2-10 Ch 2 (does not count as st), hdc in each st across. Resulting gauge swatch should measure approx 4" x 4"/10cm x 10cm. Adjust hook size if necessary to obtain correct gauge.

Stitch Glossary

Surface sl st (surface slip stitch) Make a slip knot and hold it on wrong side of fabric. Insert hook from right side of fabric to wrong side. Place slip knot on hook, draw loop to right side. Insert hook from right side to wrong side through desired stitch or space, yarn over, draw loop to right side and through loop on hook (surface slip stitch made). Working yarn will always remain on wrong side of fabric; hook will always be inserted from right side of fabric.

Notes

1. Use a separate ball of yarn for each diamond.
2. To change color, work last stitch of old color until 2 loops remain on hook. Yarn over with new color and draw through loops on hook to complete stitch. Do not cut old color; leave it to be picked up and used on next row.

Afghan

With A, ch 170.
Row 1 Hdc in 3rd ch from hook and each ch across—168 hdc.
Rows 2–16 Ch 2 (does not count as st, here and throughout), turn, hdc in each st across.
Rows 17 and 18 (see chart on next page) With A, ch 2, turn, hdc in first 41 sts; change to B, hdc in next 2 sts; change to A, hdc in next 40 sts; change to C, hdc in next 2 sts; change to A, hdc in next 40 sts; change to B, hdc in next 2 sts; change to A, hdc in last 41 sts.
Row 19 (see chart) With A, ch 2, turn, hdc in first 39 sts; change to B, hdc in next 6 sts; change to A, hdc in next 36 sts; change to C, hdc in next 6 sts; change to A, hdc in next 36 sts; change to B, hdc in next 6 sts; change to A, hdc in last 39 sts.
Rows 20–142 Work in hdc, making color changes according to chart.
Rows 143–158 Ch 2, turn, hdc in each st across. Do not fasten off.

Border

Round 1 With A, sc evenly spaced around all 4 sides of afghan, working [sc, ch 3, sc] in each corner; join with sl st in first sc.
Round 2 Ch 2 (counts as first hdc), hdc in each sc around, working [hdc, ch 3, hdc] in each corner ch-3 sp; join with sl st in top of beginning ch-2. Fasten off.
Join B with sl st in any st of Round 2.
Round 3 Ch 1, sc in each hdc around, working [sc, ch 3, sc] in each corner ch-3 sp; join with sl st in first sc. Fasten off.
Join D with sl st in any st of Round 3.
Round 4 Sl st loosely in each st around. Fasten off.

Finishing

With D, work surface sl st to create diagonal lines as shown in chart.
Weave in all ends.

Stitch Diagram

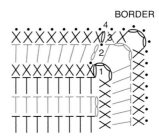

oversized argyles

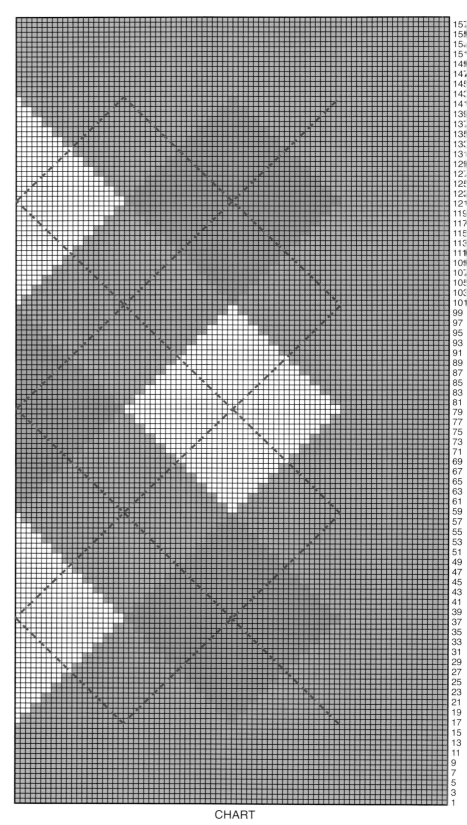

CHART KEY
☐ = hdc in A
☐ = hdc in B
☐ = hdc in C
– – – = surface crochet in D

CHART

157
155
153
151
149
147
145
143
141
139
137
135
133
131
129
127
125
123
121
119
117
115
113
111
109
107
105
103
101
99
97
95
93
91
89
87
85
83
81
79
77
75
73
71
69
67
65
63
61
59
57
55
53
51
49
47
45
43
41
39
37
35
33
31
29
27
25
23
21
19
17
15
13
11
9
7
5
3
1

boho bedspread

Materials

Yarn (4)

LC *Essentials*, 6oz/170g skeins, each approx 312yd/285m (acrylic)

3 skeins #2112 Black (A)
2 skeins #2615 Lt Celery (B)
2 skeins #2313 Aran (C)
2 skeins #2220 Butter (D)
2 skeins #2919 Barn Red (E)
1 skein #2680 Eden Green (F)
1 skein #2531 Light Plum (G)
1 skein #2690 Fusion (H)

Hook

Size I/9 (5.50mm) crochet hook *or any size to obtain correct gauge*

Additional
• Yarn needle

Measurements

Approx 66"/167.5cm wide x 72"/183cm high

Gauge

11 dc = 4"/10cm; 7 dc rows = 4¼"/11cm
Remember to check gauge for best results!

Stitch Glossary

V-st (v-stitch) Work (dc, ch 3, dc) in specified st or sp.
Shell Work 5 dc in specified st or sp.

Coverlet

With A, ch 223 loosely.
Row 1 (right side) Dc in 4th ch from hook (skipped chs count as dc), dc in next 10 chs; *V-st in next ch, dc in next 12 chs**; sk next 3 chs, dc in next 12 chs; repeat from * across, ending last repeat at **—8 ch-3 sps and 208 dc.
Row 2 Turn; sk first dc, sl st in next dc, ch 3 (counts as dc now and throughout), dc in next 11 dc; *V-st in ch-3 sp of next V-st, dc in next 12 dc**; sk next 2 dc, dc in next 12 dc; repeat from * across, ending last repeat at **. Fasten off, leaving last dc unworked.
Row 3 With right side facing, sk first dc, join B with sl st in next dc, ch 3, dc in next 11 dc; *V-st in ch-3 sp of next V-st, dc in next 12 dc**; sk next 2 dc, dc in next 12 dc; repeat from * across, ending last repeat at **. Do not fasten off, leaving last dc unworked.
Row 4 Repeat Row 2.
Rows 5–20 Repeat Rows 3 and 4, 8 more times, changing color at beginning of each odd numbered row and working 2 rows of each color in the following sequence: C, D, E, A, F, G, H, A, B.
Rows 21–92 Repeat Rows 3—20, 4 more times.
Rows 93–102 Repeat Rows 3—12. At end of last row, fasten off.

Border
Right Edge
Row 1 With right side facing, join A with sl st in bottom right-hand corner ch (3rd skipped ch at beginning of Row 1 of coverlet); working across right edge, ch 1, sc in same ch as joining; *2 sc in edge of each row, sc in top of dc or in 3rd ch of ch-3 on each row; repeat from * across—307 sc.
Row 2 Ch 1, turn; sc in first sc; *ch 2, sk next 2 sc, sc in next sc; repeat from * across—102 ch-2 sps.
Row 3 Ch 1, turn; sc in first sc; *shell in next ch-2 sp, sc in next

ch-2 sp; repeat from * across; sc in last sc—51 shells. Fasten off.

Left Edge
Row 1 With right side facing, join A with sl st in 3rd ch of beginning ch-3 on Row 102 in top left-hand corner; working across left edge, ch 1, sc in same ch as joining; *2 sc in edge of each row, sc in top of dc or in 3rd ch of ch-3 on each row; repeat from * across; sc in foundation ch at base of last dc on Row 1 of coverlet—307 sc.
Row 2 Work same as Row 2 on right edge border.
Row 3 Ch 1, turn; sc in first sc; *sc in next ch-2 sp, shell in next ch-2 sp; repeat from * across; sc in last sc—51 shells. Do not fasten off.

boho bedspread

Bottom Edge

Row 1 Ch 2, sl st in edge of last sc on Row 1 of left edge border; working in free lps of foundation chs across bottom edge; *[ch 2, sk next ch, sl st in next ch] 6 times, sk next ch, sl st in next ch; [ch 2, sk next ch, sl st in next ch] 5 times**; ch 2, sk next ch, (sl st, ch 3, sl st) in ch-3 sp; repeat from * across, ending last repeat at **; ch 2, sk last ch, sl st in edge of first sc on Row 1 of right edge border; ch 2; join with sl st in first sc on Row 3 of right edge border. Fasten off.

Top Edge

Row 1 With right side facing, join A with sl st in edge of last sc on Row 3 of right edge border; working across top edge, ch 2, sl st in edge of last sc on Row 1 of right edge border, [ch 2, sk next dc, sl st in next dc] 6 times; *ch 2, sk next dc, (sl st, ch 3, sl st) in ch-3 sp; [ch 2, sk next dc, sl st in next dc] 6 times**; ch 1, sk next dc, sl st in next dc; [ch 2, sk next dc, sl st in next dc] 5 times;

repeat from * across, ending last repeat at **; ch 2, sk last dc, sl st in edge of first sc on Row 1 of left edge border, ch 2; join with sl st in first sc on Row 3 of left edge border. Fasten off.

Finishing

Weave in all ends. Block as needed.

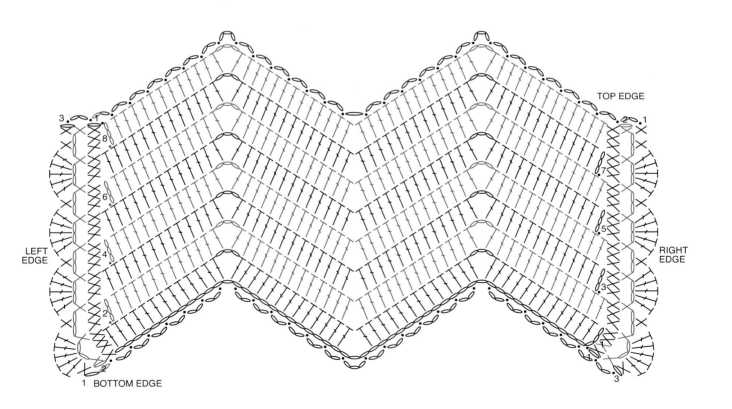

seashore afghan

Materials
Yarn [4]
TLC *Cotton Plus*, 3.5oz/100g skeins, each approx 178yd/163m
(cotton/acrylic)
6 balls #3811 Medium Blue (A)
3 balls #3810 Light Blue (B)
2 balls #3303 Tan (C)
2 balls #3100 Cream (D)
Hook
Size I/9 (5.5mm) crochet hook *or any size to obtain correct gauge*
Additional
Yarn needle

Measurements
Approx 45"/114cm wide x 58"/147cm long

Gauge
1 chevron repeat = 6"/15cm and 9 row repeat = 4"/10cm over
chevron pattern using size I/9 (5.5mm) crochet hook.
Remember to check gauge for best results!

How to make a gauge swatch
Ch 28, work Rows 1 through 9 of Afghan instructions (below).
Resulting gauge swatch should measure approx 6" x 4"/15cm x
10cm. Adjust hook size if necessary to obtain correct gauge.

Notes
Afghan is worked from top edge down to lower edge.

Afghan
With A, ch 195.
Row 1 (right side) Dc in 4th ch from hook and in next 10 ch, (dc,
ch 3, dc) in next ch, dc in next 12 ch, *sk 3 ch, dc in next 12 ch,
(dc, ch 3, dc) in next ch, dc in next 12 ch; repeat from * across—7
chevrons.
Row 2 (wrong side) Ch 1, turn, sk first dc, [sc in next dc, ch 1,
sk 1 dc] 6 times, (sc, ch 2, sc) in next ch-3 sp, [ch 1, sk 1 dc, sc
in next dc] 6 times, *sk next 2 dc, [sc in next dc, ch 1, sk 1 dc] 6
times, (sc, ch 2, sc) in next ch-3 sp, [ch 1, sk 1 dc, sc in next dc] 6
times; repeat from * across, leave turning ch unworked.
Row 3 Turn, sl st in next ch-1 sp, ch 4 (counts as dc, ch 1), sk
next sc, [dc in next ch-1 sp, ch 1, sk next sc] 5 times, (dc, ch 3,
dc) in next ch-2 sp, [ch 1, sk next sc, dc in next ch-1 sp] 6 times,
*sk next 2 sc, [dc in next ch-1 sp, ch 1, sk next sc] 6 times, (dc,
ch 3, dc) in next ch-2 sp, [ch 1, sk next sc, dc in next ch-1 sp] 6
times; repeat from * across to last sc, leave last sc unworked.
Fasten off. Join B with sl st in last dc.
Row 4 Ch 1, turn, [sc in next ch-1 sp, ch 1, sk next dc] 6 times,
(sc, ch 2, sc) in next ch-3 sp, [ch 1, sk next dc, sc in next ch-1 sp]
6 times, * sk next 2 dc, [sc in next ch-1 sp, ch 1, sk next dc] 6
times, (sc, ch 2, sc) in next ch-3 sp, [ch 1, sk next dc, sc in next
ch-1 sp] 6 times; repeat from * across.
Row 5 Ch 1, turn, sk first sc, [sc in next ch-1 sp, sc in next sc]
6 times, (sc, ch 2, sc) in next ch-2 sp, [sc in next sc, sc in next
ch-1 sp] 6 times, * sk next 2 sc, [sc in next ch-1 sp, sc in next sc]
6 times, (sc, ch 2, sc) in next ch-2 sp, [sc in next sc, sc in next
ch-1 sp] 6 times; repeat from * across to last sc, leave last sc
unworked.
Row 6 Ch 1, turn, sk first sc, [sc in next sc, ch 1, sk next sc] 6
times, (sc, ch 2, sc) in next ch-2 sp, [ch 1, sk next sc, sc in next

sc] 6 times, *sk next 2 sc, [sc in next sc, ch 1, sk next sc] 6
times, (sc, ch 2, sc) in next ch-2 sp, [ch 1, sk next sc, sc in next
sc] 6 times; repeat from * across to last sc, leave last sc unworked. Fasten off. Join C with sl st in last sc.
Row 7 Repeat Row 5.
Row 8 Ch 1, turn, sk first sc, sc in next 12 sc, (sc, ch 2, sc) in
next ch-2 sp, sc in next 12 sc, *sk 2 sc, sc in next 12 sc, (sc, ch 2,
sc) in next ch-2 sp, sc in next 12 sc; repeat from * across to last
sc, leave last sc unworked. Fasten off. Join D with sl st in last sc.
Row 9 Turn, sl st into 2nd sc, ch 4 (counts as dc, ch 1), sk next
sc, [dc in next sc, ch 1, sk next sc] 5 times, (dc, ch 3, dc) in next
ch-2 sp, [ch 1, sk next sc, dc in next sc] 6 times, *sk next 2 sc,
[dc in next sc, ch 1, sk next sc] 6 times, (dc, ch 3, dc) in next ch-2
sp, [ch 1, sk next sc, dc in next sc] 6 times; repeat from * across
to last sc, leave last sc unworked. Fasten off.
Row 10 (right side) Do not turn, join A with sl st in first ch-1
sp, ch 3, dc in next dc [dc in next ch-1 sp, dc in next dc] 5 times,
(dc, ch 3, dc) in next ch-3 sp, [dc in next dc, dc in next ch-1 sp] 6
times, *sk next 2 dc, [dc in next ch-1 sp, dc in next dc] 6 times,
(dc, ch 3, dc) in next ch-3 sp, [dc in next dc, dc in next ch-1 sp] 6
times; repeat from * across.
Rows 11-120 Repeat Rows 2-10 twelve more times, then repeat
Rows 2 and 3. Do not fasten off A.

Side edging
Row 1 (right side) With A, ch 1, do not turn, working in ends of
rows along side edge, 3 sc in end of first dc row, *sc in end of
next sc row, 2 sc in end of next 2 dc rows, sc in end of next 5 sc
rows, 2 sc in end of next dc row; repeat from * across to last 2
rows, sc in end of next sc row, 3 sc in end of last dc row—163 sc.
Rows 2-5 Ch 1, turn, sc in each sc across. Fasten off.
With right side facing, join A with sl st in base of ch-3 turning ch
of Row 1.
Row 1 (right side) Ch 1, 3 sc in ch-3 sp of turning ch, *sc in end
of next sc row, 2 sc in end of next dc row, sc in end of next 5 sc
rows, 2 sc in end of next 2 dc rows; repeat from * across to last 2

rows, sc in end of next sc row, 3 sc in end of last dc row—163 sc.
Rows 2-5 Ch 1, turn, sc in each sc across.
Fasten off.

Border

With right side facing and foundation ch edge at top, join A with sl st in 3rd sc of last row of right side.

Working across right edge to top Ch 1, (sc, ch 2, sc) in same sc, * sk 1 sc, (sc, ch 2, sc) in next sc; repeat from * across, ending sk last sc.

Working in ends of rows of right edge (sc, ch 3, sc) in corner, [sk 1 row, (sc, ch 2, sc) in end of next row] twice.

Working in free loops of foundation ch across top edge [ch 2, sk next ch, sl st in next ch] 6 times, sk next ch, sl st in next ch, [ch 2, sk 1 ch, sl st in next ch] 5 times, *ch 2, sk next ch, (sl st, ch 4, sl st) in next ch-3 sp, [ch 2, sk 1 ch, sl st in next ch] 6 times, sk next ch, sl st in next ch, [ch 2, sk 1 ch, sl st in next ch] 5 times; repeat from * across.

Working in ends of rows of left edge ch 2, (sc, ch 2, sc) in end of next row, sk 1 row, (sc, ch 2, sc) in end of next row, sk 1 row, (sc, ch 3, sc) in corner.

Working across left edge to lower edge * sk 1 sc, (sc, ch 2, sc) in

next sc; repeat from * across, ending sk last sc.

Working in ends of rows of left edge (sc, ch 3, sc) in corner, [sk 1 row, (sc, ch 2, sc) in end of next row] twice.

Working across lower edge ch 2, sl st in next ch-1 sp, [ch 2, sk next dc, sl st in next ch-1 sp] 5 times, ch 2, sk next dc, (sl st, ch 4, sl st) in next ch-3 sp, [ch 2, sk next dc, sl st in next ch-1 sp] 6 times, * sk next 2 dc, sl st in next ch-1 sp, [ch 2, sk next dc, sl st in next ch-1 sp] 5 times, ch 2, sk next dc, (sl st, ch 4, sl st) in next ch-3 sp, [ch 2, sk next dc, sl st in next ch-1 sp] 6 times; repeat from * across.

Working in ends of rows of right edge ch 2, (sc, ch 2, sc) in end of next row, sk 1 row, (sc, ch 2, sc) in end of next row, sk next row, (sc, ch 3, sc) in corner, sk next sc; join with sl st in beg sc. Fasten off.

Finishing

Weave in all ends.

BORDER

5 3 1
119

FIRST SIDE EDGING

8
6
4
2
4 2

120
118

SECOND SIDE EDGING

10
9
7
5
3
1
1 3 5

elegant filet afghan

Materials

Yarn (4)

RED HEART *Soft Yarn*, 5oz/140g balls, each approx 256yd/234m (acrylic)

7 balls #9518 Teal

Hook

Size I/9 (5.5mm) crochet hook or any size to obtain correct gauge

Additional

Yarn needle

Measurements

approx 50"/127cm wide x 58"/147cm long

Gauge

15 sts (7 blocks) and 7 rows = 4"/10cm over Filet pattern using size I/9 (5.5mm) crochet hook.

Remember to check gauge for best results!

How To Make A Gauge Swatch

Ch 18.

Row 1 Dc in 6th ch from hook (counts as first open block), [ch 1, sk 1 ch, dc in next ch] across—7 blocks.

Rows 2-7 Work in Filet pattern. Fasten off.

Resulting gauge swatch should measure approx 4" x 4"/10cm x 10cm. Adjust hook size if necessary to obtain correct gauge.

Stitch Glossary

Pattern Stitch

Worked on an odd number of sts.

Filet Pattern Ch 4 (counts as dc, ch 1), turn, sk first dc and next ch-1 sp, dc in next dc, ch 1, *sk next ch-1 sp, dc in next dc, ch 1; repeat from * across, ending dc in 3rd ch of turning ch.

To decrease in pattern (1 open block decreased each side) Ch 1, turn, sl st in first ch-1 sp, sl st in next dc, ch 4 (counts as dc, ch 1), sk next ch-sp, dc in next dc, continue in Filet pattern according to chart across to last open block; leave last open block unworked.

To inc in pattern (1 open block inc each side) Ch 5, dc in first dc (at base of turning ch), ch 1, sk next ch-sp, dc in next dc, continue in Filet pattern according to chart, ending (dc, ch 1, dtr) in turning ch.

Afghan

Ch 158.

Note Refer to chart on next page to work Afghan as follows:

. Read right side rows from right to left.

. Read wrong side rows from left to right.

. For each open block on chart: Work ch 1, sk ch-1 sp, dc in next dc.

. For each solid block on chart: Work dc in ch-1 sp, dc in next dc.

Instructions for the first few rows are given in detail below.

Row 1 (right side) Dc in 6th ch from hook (counts as first open block), [ch 1, sk 1 ch, dc in next ch] across—77 blocks.

Row 2 (inc) Ch 5, turn, dc in first dc (one open block inc), sk first ch-1 sp, dc in next dc, [dc in next ch-1 sp, dc in next dc] across to last open block, ch 1, sk next ch-1 sp, (dc, ch 1, dtr) in 4th ch of turning ch (one open block inc)—79 blocks.

Row 3 (inc) Ch 5, turn, dc in first dc (one open block inc), ch 1, sk first ch-1 sp, dc in next dc (1 open block made), *dc in next 8 sts (4 closed blocks made), ch 1, sk next dc, dc in next dc (1 open

elegant filet afghan

lock made), dc in next 4 dc (2 closed blocks made), ch 1, sk next
c, dc in next dc (1 open block made), dc in next 6 dc (3 closed
locks made), [ch 1, sk next dc, dc in next dc] 5 times (5 open
locks made), dc in next 4 dc, [ch 1, sk next dc, dc in next dc] 5
mes, dc in next 6 dc, ch 1, sk 1 dc, dc in next dc, dc in next 4 dc,
h 1, sk 1 dc, dc in next dc, dc in next 8 sts*, [ch 1, sk 1 dc, dc in
ext dc] 9 times; repeat from * to *, ch 1, sk next ch-1 sp, (dc, ch
, dtr) in 4th ch of turning ch (one open block inc)—81 blocks.

Row 4 Ch 4 (counts as dc, ch 1), turn, sk first dc and ch-sp, dc in
ext dc, *dc in next 6 dc, [ch 1, sk 1 st, dc in next dc] 5 times, dc
n next 4 sts, [ch 1, sk 1 st, dc in next dc] 6 times, dc in next ch 1
p, dc in next dc, [ch 1, sk 1 st, dc in next dc] 2 times, dc in next
h-1 sp, dc in next dc, [ch 1, sk 1 st, dc in next dc] 6 times, dc in
ext 4 dc, [ch 1, sk 1 st, dc in next dc] 5 times, dc in next 6 sts*,

[ch 1, sk 1 st, dc in next dc] 7 times; repeat from * to *, ch 1, dc
in 4th ch of turning ch.
Rows 5–97 Continue in Filet pattern according to chart.
Do not fasten off.

FINISHING
Edging
Round 1 Work sc evenly spaced around all edges of Afghan,
increasing in corners as necessary; join with sl st in first sc.
Round 2 Working from left to right, [rev sc in next st, ch 1, sk
next st] around; join with sl st in first st. Fasten off.
Weave in all ends.

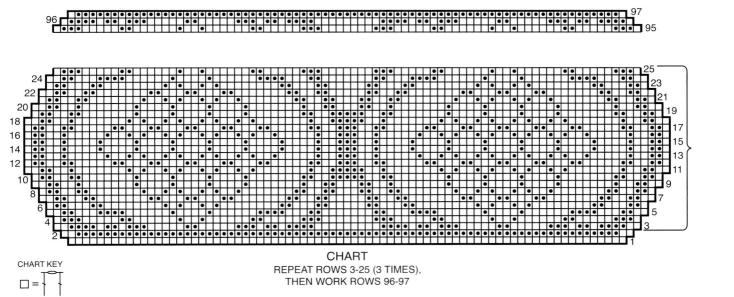

CHART
REPEAT ROWS 3-25 (3 TIMES),
THEN WORK ROWS 96-97

CHART KEY

□ =

▣ =

rose garden afghan

Materials

Yarn (4)

TLC *Essentials*, 6oz/170g skeins, each approx 312yd/285m (acrylic)
- 5 skeins #2313 Aran

Hook

Size I/9 (5.5mm) crochet hook *or any size to obtain correct gauge*

Additional
- Yarn needle

Measurements

Approx 42"/106.5cm x 63"/160cm

Gauge

15 dc + 7 rows = 4"/10cm
Remember to check gauge for best results!

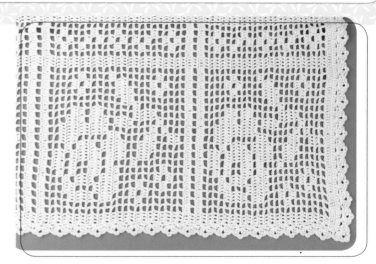

Stitch Glossary

Open mesh Ch 2, sk next 2 sts, dc in next dc.
Closed mesh Dc in next 3 sts.
Shell Work (2 dc, ch 2, 2 dc) in specified st or sp.

Afghan

Ch 144 loosely.

Row 1 (right side) Working in back bar of chs, dc in 4th ch from hook (sk chs count as dc), dc in each rem ch across—142 dc (47 closed mesh). Ch 3 (counts as dc on next row now and through-out), turn.

Row 2 Dc in next 3 dc (closed mesh made); *[ch 2, sk next 2 sts, dc in next dc] 19 times (19 open mesh made), dc in next 3 dc (closed mesh made)*; [ch 2, sk next 2 sts, dc in next dc] 5 times (5 open mesh made), dc in next 3 dc (closed mesh made); repeat from * to * once—43 open mesh and 4 closed mesh. Ch 3, turn.

Rows 3—27 Work open and closed mesh following chart. Odd numbered rows are read from right to left and even numbered rows are read from left to right on chart. At end of each row, ch 3, turn.

Rows 28—103 Repeat Rows 2—27 two times more, then repeat Rows 2—25 once more. At end of last row, ch 1, turn.

Row 104 Sc in each dc across—142 sc. Fasten off.

Bottom Row With wrong side facing, join with sc in free lps of 3rd sk ch at beginning of Row 1, sc in free lps of each foundation ch across—142 sc. Ch 1, turn.

Edging

Round 1 (right side) Working across bottom, sc in first sc; *ch 2, sk next 2 sc, sc in next sc; *repeat from * to * across, ending with ch 2, sk next 2 sc, (sc, ch 2, sc) in last sc (corner ch-2 sp made); working across side, ch 1, sc in top of first dc on side; **ch 1, sc in top of next dc on side**; repeat from ** to ** across, ending with ch 1, sk top of last dc, (sc, ch 2, sc) in first sc on top row (corner ch-2 sp made); repeat from * across top and other side, beginning other side with ch 1, sk top of first dc, sc in top of next dc on side and ending other side with ch 1, sc in same

sc as first sc worked, ch 2 (corner ch-2 sp made)—47 ch-2 sps on top and bottom, 103 ch-1 sps on each side and 4 corner ch-2 sps. Join with sl st in first sc.

Round 2 (Sl st, ch 1, sc) in next ch-2 sp; *shell in next ch-2 sp, sc in next ch-2 sp; repeat from * across bottom; (3 dc, ch 2, 3 dc) in corner ch-2 sp (corner shell made); working across side, sc in next ch-1 sp; **sk next sc, shell in next sc, sk next ch-1 sp, sc in next ch-1 sp; repeat from ** across side; (3 dc, ch 2, 3 dc) in corner ch-2 sp (corner shell made)***; working across top, sc in next ch-2 sp; repeat from * across top and other side, ending at ***—23 shells on top and bottom, 34 shells on each side and 4 corner shells. Join with sl st in first sc.

Round 3 *Ch 3, (sl st, ch 3, sl st) in ch-2 sp of next shell, ch 3, sl st in next sc; repeat from * around, working [ch 3, sk next 2 dc, sl st in next dc, ch 2, (sl st, ch 3, sl st) in ch-2 sp, ch 2, sl st in next dc, ch 3, sk next 2 dc, sl st in next sc] in each corner shell. Join with sl st in joining sl st. Fasten off.

Finishing

Weave in all ends. Block lightly.

rose garden afghan

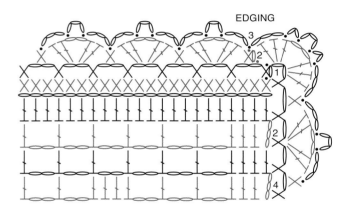

EDGING

CHART KEY

□ =

⊡ =

CHART KEY

□ = Open mesh: Ch 2,
skip next 2 sts, dc in next st.

⊡ = Closed mesh: Dc in next 3 sts.

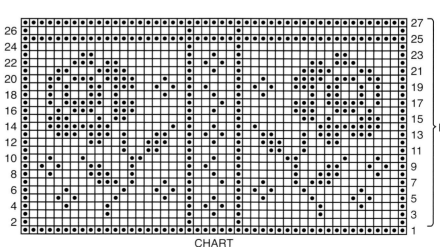

CHART

REPEAT